They Bring it On Themselves

ISBN 978-0-9918395-0-6

Snapdragon Press
Whitehorse, Yukon
Canada

Contents

Dreaming, or Awake

I watched the stars last night;
now the sky is dark again.
The stars were smaller, duller,
as if the Big Bang were pulling them away.

The dog had a twisting fit last night.
I held her in my arms. I woke to her nose
before I knew I was dreaming.
The hollows in her eye-bones

are real, her slow-hipped conquer
of the couch, though she's only three.
The bad haircut I gave myself is real,
a teenage mistake at forty.

A visit to a hairdresser
is two lines of a vet's bill. A drive
to town is time for tummy-rubbing.
The stars are fixed; Earth falls.

The Abattoir Worker's Wife

At the abattoir, the workers switch off
the throat cutters and reach to unclasp
the feet of the chickens hanging upside
down. Some of the birds die at the touch
of warm broad hands.

The worker on his break puts down
his ham sandwich, lifts eight birds into
a crate that held eighty when they came in.
He drives home slowly, braking
gently at traffic lights.

His wife, who made his sandwiches,
is out when he gets home.
She's taken the pig from the fridge
to bury in the cemetery. He carries
the crate carefully into the house.

His knees crack as he crouches to invite
the chickens onto the living room
carpet. When his wife returns,
they decide to give them
the spare room for now.

They spread newspaper sheets on the floor,
fill margarine tubs with water.
She takes them sunflower seeds
she finds in a kitchen cupboard
then goes back downstairs for a cup of tea.

They agree it's quite nice black.
He isn't sure if they'll have to pay
for the operations to relieve the pain
of shorn off beaks and broken wings.
She says if they do, they'll find the money.

They discuss how many cows
could fit in the back yard. The abattoir
worker wonders about sheep.
His wife smiles. She says
she's always wanted a lamb.

Idling

On the way to the bus-stop
I pass a pick-up truck at the mall
with a moose rack on the back,
wishboned by its skull,
a cheap black chain looped
through one eye socket.

A khaki ball cap is on the dash.
The truck is red and idling.
Hunters respect the animal
they're about to shoot.
It takes more guts to respect what's left:
unfastened, enduring bones.

Horses at Knockdarroch

After a curry last night we probably
parked the Fiesta beside two of them
in the dark. Outside animals. Quiet.
Horses, standing massive in the morning.

Through the skyless window in this rented
bedroom only snow, firs, fences, grass,
until I sit low on the painted window seat,
see clouds flattening billows of pink mist,

as if they're trying to pack up a tent.
If I understood how horses stand the cold
I might know why humans save them
for riding instead of eating, because

cows stand in the dark by cars too.
Now, a girl in jodhpurs gets out of Daddy's
green Range Rover. He leaves her
in the paddock beyond the field.

I watch her walk the largest horse
in wide circles, imagining a broad back,
a thick spine, fingers fused into hooves,
waiting for the weight of leathered cow.

Biology Lesson

I was in the biology class
that was supposed to make it all make sense,
when Mr Watson drew God on the
blackboard and said death was good.

Everything alive would die
and decompose. It was better
to be buried than be burned.
Everything killed something

else in order to survive.
I called out *I didn't*;
I was a herbivore.
He told me I'd get ill;

I wasn't a cow or a rabbit.
The class thought that was funny.
I sketched a rabbit on the cover
of my exercise book.

I had a rabbit at home
with a tumour on his spine
who I was keeping alive.
On Sunday, my mother made me

help her dig the garden.
She sat back on the heels
of her rubber boots, muddying
the backside of her old blue trousers.

She said: Last week I stuck a fork
into the soil and heard a scream.
She'd stabbed a frog.
She definitely heard it scream.

I was the first person she'd told.
She'd put the body in the compost.
She wished now she'd buried it
where the daffodils grew.

We watched a mosquito bite
her forearm, blood ballooning
in its abdomen. It looked too heavy
to fly but it reached the raspberries.

If my mother had squashed it, her
own blood would have smeared her skin.
She started digging with the fork
but I dug with blunt fingers.

I was the heroine in a film, mud-smeared
face, long black hair flowing,
a silhouette against a thunderous sky,
shouting: Nobody else dies here!

Burns Supper

Every year on Burns Night,
my heart was broken by a shining haggis.
Cleaned, scalded, soaked and salted
before it was baked. Addressed, fingered,

sliced, gutted and digested afterwards
by people of sometimes surprisingly
diverse political persuasions in one room.
I leant on one thick soundproofing palm

to protect at least one eardrum from the
barrage that piped the inside-out stomach in.
I preferred the blast of bagpipes far and high
on a Glen Coe hill. Indoors, they were the mace

that stunned the lamb who donated its heart and lungs.
Onions, oatmeal, coriander, nutmeg.
It must have happened: a lamb's organs sewn up,
thick threaded, inside its own mother's stomach.

Shmeat

The professor told the reporter no one had
tasted it yet, meat made in the laboratory:
pig cells grown in a solution of nutrients.
He didn't know one of his scientists had taken
a lump home for a fry-up and judged it
good enough to eat, though somewhat gluey.
It was she who suggested giving the meat
a work-out. No one liked a flabby dinner,
preferring the taste of cattle driven across the range.
She designed the apparatus on the back
of a junk mail envelope as she sat in her kitchen
chewing chops slathered in brown sauce.
She drew rubber clasps and pulleys.
For now, they were using blood
from animal foetuses to feed the cells
but the professor was working
on a synthetic solution.
The vegetarians who wouldn't eat
anything with eyes would be no problem;
this meat was blind from birth.
The egg-refusers would be confused.
The vegans would miss the point.
The professor, being Jewish, had never
eaten a pig. Surely this fleshy inflammation
could not be classified as porcine; it would
never grow split hooves or ruminate.
Staying late one night, when everyone
had gone, he sliced off a sliver with a scalpel,
put it in his empty lunch box and took it home.

At the Aquarium

Perhaps all the people streaming past
make Pacific herring think they're moving,
balled in a perpetual shoal
inside a lidded cylinder,
a giant jar of silver spinning fish.

Over children's heads and hands,
above the spikes of their voices,
I watch one herring flow contrarily,
nose up until it divides into purple bubbles,
a dark eye drifting out of its own light.

The whole shoal changes direction as I watch,
though I don't see it. I was observing
how only the rear of each fish moves.
There's plenty of space around this core of sea
but I can't get past the sound of them.

You're on to the five-hearted hagfish
that's down on the fake sea bed, sliding
into a dead fish's mouth and anus,
like a turd pushing the wrong way,
to eat it from the inside.

You remind me to be thankful for the hagfish
and – your favourite – the Sexton beetle:
the waste disposer and the undertaker.
I look back at the herring trap, still hearing
the dizzy cram of the eternally shoaled.

A man and boy eat chips from a plastic tray
in front of Quadra Island. In Australia,
two parents crouch to double phone-snap
their children glassed and laughing
at spitting whitebarred gobies.

14

In the Amazon rainforest
I grab the finger of a cecropia leaf.
At last there's no glass. I don't move
when water drips on my head.
Sloths – dark burls above us – eat vegetables.

They take at least a week to digest a meal.
In the Strait of Georgia, the label back there
said, more than ninety per cent of herring
are caught for the eggs inside them.
When we leave, I avoid the pot of fish.

On the bus I hear them still, squashed
in that cylinder, sick with endless circling.
As soon as I'm in wifi range, I Google Pacific herrings.
It says they live in shoals all their lives.
All I'm hearing is water stirred in a glass.

Fur Bearer

She tells me she needs a nose peg
for the smell. Beavers are sticky,
opened and scraping.

She's learning to peel the pelt
from stubborn muscle towards
the armpits, groin and spine.

She'll need a circular board
to stretch not tear it, two-inch nails
one inch apart all the way round.

She's caught more wolf and coyote
than beaver this winter, she's no idea
why. There goes the definite article,

dropped in the snow like a glove.
I don't tell her I saw it fall.
Let her hand get cold.

I see a wolf cub snatch the thumb
of the glove while his mother cuts
through spruce to taste a smell.

The cub drops the glove at the thud
of steel on his mother's throat.
He suckles as she dies.

Trap lines aren't actually lines,
not wires stretched taut to trip.
There are gaps between the traps.

The animals who walk through
the spaces would never know,
but for that sticky smell.

16

Cat and Mouse

The charity tin-shaker has a nice smile
but I'm too busy leading myself out
of temptation on Main Street
to walk his way, until I spot
the pink ribbon on his can.

Got a minute for cancer research?
A donation?
A bequest is best.

How many mouse mutations
to the pound, I want to know.
How many monkey mammaries
would a monthly debit fund?
How many dog disembowelments
is each donation worth?

His face is unwritten,
like the cheque
that will stay in my purse.
He's *never been asked that before.*
He doesn't tell me about
his sister/mother/girlfriend like he should,
or remind me of my best friend's
reconstructed breasts.

I give him my authentic smile.
I even say I'm sorry
because he's not the one
who stole Tabitha
when I was eight.
He doesn't give cats
cancer or AIDS,
or test medicines for headaches
they only get when holes
are drilled into their skulls.

Country Life

Flip on your cap, whistle the dog.
Kiss me goodbye, mouth open.

Why won't you share your English
country ways with me?

If you reach the beeches without
looking back, I'm going to follow you.

Your little dog knows I'm here but she's
not telling. We walk for fifteen minutes

to a sudden mossy stop. I hide behind an oak
as a stand of flat-capped men surround you.

The dusk loudens sounds as mist magnifies
mountains. A few human words set off

the yapping. Terriers sniff the holes.
Larger dogs stand back as men grip shovels.

Men yip, the terriers go down.
I hear a frantic subterranean squeal.

A screech and your dog is out,
muzzle ripped back from grubby teeth.

You reach past your screaming dog
to tug at a bulky body, shabby-furred.

You raise your spade, crack it down
on the badger's black and white striped crown.

I'm clamped by the stench of musk and blood.
I'll never open my mouth for you again.

They Bring it on Themselves

The headline said
Polar bears may endanger humans as climate changes

They killed the wolf at the dump, the officer said
because it didn't show any fear of humans

The police said they shot and killed two cows running loose
because they *were aggressive and a threat to residents*

The restaurant advertisement said
Enjoy your place at the top of the food chain

Kill two birds with one stone
Flog a dead horse
A bird in the hand is worth two in the bush
Curiosity killed the cat
Nothing on Earth can bring it back

The Mosquito and the Whale

Little Joe Tuckfield, what did you do?
Charlie Brower sent you to the delta with a year's supplies
and you came back and told the truth.
You said the bowhead whales were as thick as bees.

You brought some whalebone back to prove it,
so the ladies could have hoops in their skirts
and the gentlemen could have whips in their hands.
Little Joe Tuckfield, what did you do?

In eighteen-eighty-nine for almost twenty years
they shot their barbs from harpoon guns
on the bow, through sleek skin, deep into the blubber,
detonating fuses because that's how humans do things.

I remember, as a child, finding out there was whale oil
in shoe polish. I didn't stop my father polishing seven pairs
of shoes each Sunday night. I laughed each time
he put one of his shoes in a pair with one of mine.

The bloody water, a wooden beam through a hole in her head,
her giant slick body chained to the starboard side.
Next, boarding her corpse to ram in the ripping hook,
peeling thick blankets of blubber, hacking off her head.

Now to the deck. Six-hour shifts for three days or as long
as it took. Boiling the blubber, pouring hot oil into barrels.
The stench and slither of whale on every skin and morsel.
Sometimes they took the baleen and discarded the carcass.

I don't polish my shoes any more. I don't wear seals
or cows. I don't eat caribou. I can't kill a mosquito;
I let it suck my blood and fly away. Why do I want
to go to a barren, sea-soaked island where whales

and souls were speared by whalers and missionaries?
Why do I long to crouch to touch the tundra vetches
and forget-me-nots, taste the Beaufort Sea and breathe
in a place where everyone must kill in order to stay?

958 000 000 411 618

I

About the size of a long grain of rice,
the microchip lies across a spruce needle
under an aspen leaf,
delivered to the forest floor
well before the snow
in a twisted defecation that was soft
before it was hard, whitened, desiccated.
The fur in it was never visibly orange,
more the colour of frayed rope.

At the back of the neck
between the shoulder blades
on the dorsal midline
is where it came from,
injected by a vet in Scotland,
from there by air to Canada.

Bioglass passes smoothly
through a coyote's digestive system.
Chip, core, capacitor in tact, uncracked.
It may lie there, fallen in the ripping.
I may pass it each day with the dog,
unscanned.

II

The coyote who ate the microchip
may have been eaten by a wolf.
Or a raven ate the coyote's remains,
flying the microchip
farther into the forest. Or
the raven, standing on top of a lamppost
gurgling and plunking, pooed the microchip
to the road where a Honda Civic ran it over,
pressed it uncracked into the pavement,
soft on a hot day. The road re-surfaced
a few years later, the microchip,
sedimented in landfill,
eventually excavated by a future race,
human or otherwise.

Conibear

There's a wolf in the woodshed,
as we sit down to supper, and a lynx.
Stretched from a beam by yellow rope
the wolf's tail stuck to its legs with blood,
the lynx's stub a knob to twist the corpse.
I'm told they're there by the friends
I'm visiting; I haven't been to look.
My cat is large and long. I carry him
sometimes flopped over my shoulder
like a rolled-up rug. Their golden retriever
leans against my knees.
As I eat, I smooth his silky ears.
He goes with them to the trap line,
thirty miles from the highway into the bush.
I don't know what type of trap they use
but I bet it's the conibear.
The body gripper.
The squashing can take days.
I take another mouthful
and stroke their dog's sleek fur.

Something is Rotten

The squirrel got in
because I didn't get round
to sealing the soffits.
The cat got out
because I didn't try
hard enough to stop it.
So it's true the spot growing
on my bedroom ceiling
is my fault
because the squirrel made a nest
and the cat ate the squirrel
and the baby squirrels
who starved to death
are now decomposing
and I can't sleep
because of that spot,
that upside down stained sheet
stretched over my head.

Acknowledgements

Thank you to Christopher R Burn for writing *Herschel Island Qikiqtaryuk: A Natural and Cultural History* and to the MacBride Museum and Steve Slade of Arts in the Park in Whitehorse, Yukon, whose collaborations inspired me to write The Mosquito and the Whale. Thank you to *subTerrain* for publishing Biology Lesson and to Mansfield Press for publishing a version of Something is Rotten. Thank you to everyone everywhere who has ever done anything to help an animal.

About the Author

Joanna Lilley lives in Whitehorse, Yukon with her husband, cat and dog. She has lived north of the sixtieth parallel since 2006 when she emigrated to Canada from the UK. Her poetry collection, *The Fleece Era*, is forthcoming from Brick Books in spring 2014. Joanna has worried about animals all her life and hopes this small book of poems may help them a little.

www.joannalilley.blogspot.ca

www.ingramcontent.com/pod-product-compliance
Lightning Source LLC
Chambersburg PA
CBHW020038040426
42331CB00031B/983